# A Coarser French Course

# A Coarser French Course

Alexis Maitland Hudson

Wolfe Publishing Ltd
10 Earlham Street
London WC2

Made and Printed in England by
C. Nicholls & Company Limited
at the Philips Park Press
Manchester   M11 4AU

To Janey

# ACKNOWLEDGEMENTS

I should like to thank the following people without whose help, encouragement and inspiration the writing of this book would not have been possible:

Jane Williams
Jill Angood
Rosamund Day

Andrew Jones
Paul Baskerville
Peter Wolfe
John d'Arcy Dean
Tev Chaldecott
Bertolt Brecht
Barry McKenzie

Jaki Goux
Monette Monédières
Marie-Thérèse Pougeon
Albertine Sarrazin

François Laroque
Jean-Michel Goux
Alain Fiabon
Guy Troiville
René Pougeon
Yves-Henri de France

my parents and, finally, to Lloyd's Bank, whose demands have been germinal to the early completion of the work.

A.P.M.H.
10/3/70

# CONTENTS

**Appendices**

# INTRODUCTION

For years now we have been the victims of a subtle plot on the part of the compilers of Phrase Books and French Courses to prevent us from communicating with the Frog in the street on anything but the most limited plane. If you have not noticed this vicious attempt to stultify the Briton abroad, let me expose it for you.

Firstly, we are taught stiff, rigid grammar. Thereby making us sound like badly programmed computers. This is horrendous enough in itself.

But secondly, we are provided with a pitifully inadequate vocabulary, which ensures that anything we are able to say is shatteringly boring or abjectly matter-of-fact.

And as a direct result of these factors, we are forced to converse in such a way as to convince whoever we are addressing that our grasp of the Froggy vernacular is pitiful and outrageously old-fashioned. For example, is anyone really interested if your auntie's pen is on uncle's desk? Is your tailor rich? Does it really matter if Peter's garden is bigger than John's rhubarb patch?

After this exposure, it remains only to try to bridge the gap between these outdated forms and more valid conversation. In short, to invigorate the worn-out set phrases, which have plagued the British traveller for years and which have reduced his continental sorties

11

to a series of traumatic scenes of enervating non-comprehension, resulting in the inevitable. Namely, shouting at the sods loudly and in the mother-tongue. Are we going to let these Froggy chappies gloat over our disability any longer? Have they forgotten who won the battle of Agincourt?

This book attempts to bridge this gap, at least in part, and to provide some forms and vocabulary which will enable you to get through to these Gallic fiends, and tell them what it's all about in language and phraseology that will dissociate us from the hysterical, fuddy-duddy bondage of "Pahlay voo fronsay?".

Neither the vocabulary nor the grammar is entirely definitive, but they do provide a firm basis for what I shall call "Coarse French", namely a closer approximation to French as she is spoke most of the time. I have assumed a good basic knowledge of the language for my reader, and those with G.C.E. "O" level should find no difficulty with the text. No longer will the British traveller in the fair land of France be obliged to listen to abuse in stoic silence, unable to reply because of his defective knowledge of this area of language.

But here a word of warning: the Frenchman is a volatile being, prone to outbursts of raucous indignation at the slightest provocation and possessed of a fragile Ego. Hence, I suggest you exercise especial care in the use of the Appendix on Abuse. This Appendix is primarily intended as a passive vocabulary, so you may be certain of what that greasy individual

12

just called you. Use it if you must, but do so with discretion and remember that his abusive vocabulary is probably better than yours, once he gets going. However, you will have surprise on your side. After all he won't be expecting a reply.

An element of caution is necessary, in fact, with most of the vocabulary in this book, precisely because it is different from the run-of-the-mill, "Can you direct me to the nearest salt-mine?" sort, with which we are all familiar. The words in this book are all familiar, if not actually vulgar, and should be regarded as such. And although we wish to detumesce the stiff upper lip, we don't want to overcompensate. Whereas a young Frog will be impressed if you tell him to keep his cool, his parents may not be wildly chuffed if you tell them that you're going to nip round the corner for a swift jar and a Gallic packet of crisps.

Summing up then, the idea behind this work is to soften up the bookish French we are all fobbed off with, and thus to divorce us from the Victorian traveller worried about the effects of lightning on his postillion, and the creases in his plus-fours. The danger lies in inopportune use of this new vocabulary. In paragraph 24 I have tried to indicate certain keywords which will help you to gauge the tone of conversations and tell you when to lapse into slang. Do bear this in mind, after all, you don't want to appear a yob, do you?

# BASICS

There are certain features of Coarse French which are fundamental and require some explanation.

## (i) Elision

There is a tendency, as in spoken English, to run certain common pairs of words together to produce a single sound, and in so doing to omit certain functional entities, notably **ne**, from the sentence.

Thus, "*tu as*" becomes "*t'as*"; "*je suis*" becomes "*chuis*" and "*je ne sais pas*" becomes "*ché pas*". This is important for two reasons: one, without foreknowledge of these forms, you run the risk of not understanding what is being said in the coarse language, and two, if you use coarse expressions without employing coarse forms, you are going to sound funny. While no one will be surprised in coarse conversation if you say:

Chuis pas venu voir des conneries pareilles.

the same vocabulary used in a literary form would sound bizarre in the extreme:

Je ne suis pas venu voir . . . etc. §12b

and this would only be said with specific comic intentions.

Generally speaking, the examples given in the text are in their literary, or quasi-literary form. This is done to make them more easily comprehensible. However, before you use them conversationally, remember to make the necessary elisions.

e.g.

Je ne peux pas bouquiner longtemps (§26(ii))

becomes

Ch'peux pas . . . etc.

However, such elisions are not always possible:

e.g.

Laquelle veux-tu draguer? (§45(a))

and so you must use your own discretion about them. I list below some very common contracted forms, which will give you a guide to the mechanism behind them, and I would refer you to 42–44, 52–60, 61(c) and (d).

| Literary form | Contraction |
|---|---|
| tu as | t'as |
| je suis | chuis |
| je ne sais pas | ché pas |
| je ne crois pas | ch'crois pas |
| il y a | y'a |
| il y avait | y'avait |
| cette | c'tte |
| c'était | c'té |
| je te casse | che t'casse |

15

## (ii) 3 Verbs

Coarse French possesses one very and two quite overworked verbs. They are **foutre, filer** and **baiser.**

**Foutre:** See Section I§I.

**Filer:** This has two main areas of meaning, *to give* and *to depart*.

e.g.

Tu me files un clope?

*Have you got a straight, man?*

J'ai filé à tout berzingue.

*I took off like a bat out of hell.*

**Baiser:** In a way which can only be described as typically French, the meaning of **baiser** has developed from *to kiss* to *to copulate*. However, like its English equivalents, it does have connotations of bad luck and mechanical failure.

e.g.

C'est baisé!

*It's all screwed up!*

J'étais baisé.

*I was screwed blind.*

It remains only to commit you to the grammar sections which embody the bulk of this work, and which will provide you with the basis for the Vocabulary Lists and Appendices.

# Grammar

## I CONJUGATION OF VERBS

**1.** Coarse French shares a basic vocabulary with the literary language and the conjugation of such verbs is unchanged and quite in accordance with written usage. However, it possesses a wide range of its own verbs, often borrowed from the literary language and imbued with new meaning and scope of application, and these exhibit certain anomalies. It is the conjugation of these verbs that concerns us here. Let us take an example:

**Foutre:** The dictionary definition of this verb is *to stick* or *stuff*. The Coarse Language has taken it over and uses it for virtually any action. It is most used as a substitute for *faire* or *mettre* and in other contexts it has some rather more basic connexions with stuffing. Like most coarse verbs it has a defective conjugation and by conjugating it fully, as it exists in the Coarse Language, we shall see what the anomalies are. They will then be considered more carefully in the next section.

17

**Present Indicative:** formed from the stem fou-plus s, s, t, tons, tez, tent.

| | |
|---|---|
| je fous | nous foutons |
| tu fous | vous foutez |
| il fout | ils foutent |

**Passé Composé:** formed from the past participle and the present indicative of avoir.

| | |
|---|---|
| j'ai foutu | nous avons foutu |
| tu as foutu | vous avez foutu |
| il a foutu | ils ont foutu |

**Imperfect:** formed from the stem fout- plus ais, ais, ait, ions, iez, aient.

| | |
|---|---|
| je foutais | nous foutions |
| tu foutais | vous foutiez |
| il foutait | ils foutaient |

**Future:** formed from the present infinitive and the present indicative of aller.

| | |
|---|---|
| je vais foutre | nous allons foutre |
| tu vas foutre | vous allez foutre |
| il va foutre | ils vont foutre |

**Present subjunctive:** formed from the stem fout- plus e, es, e, ions, iez, ent.

| | |
|---|---|
| que je foute | que nous foutions |
| que tu foutes | que vous foutiez |
| qu'il foute | qu'ils foutent |

**2.** All coarse verbs lose their colloquial significance outside these five tenses and revert back to their dictionary definitions.

**3.** The coarse verb is most commonly used in the 1st, 2nd, and 3rd person singular and the 2nd person plural. Some very common verbs, such as foutre, filer, se tirer, do occur in all persons, but for the less frequent verbs it is as well to remember that the 1st and 3rd person plural, in particular, if used, will have undesirable overtones of comic Bathos which may cause embarrassment.

# II  USE OF TENSES

**4.** In this section we shall consider how coarse verbs are used and any difficulties that arise from the defective conjugation.

## 5. Present

(a) There are a group of common coarse verbs which do not have any meaning, or have a different meaning in the present tense:

| | |
|---|---|
| chiper | |
| piquer | *pinch, nick* |
| se cuiter | |
| prendre une cuite | *get smashed, knotted, tight* |
| louper | *miss (a train etc.)* |
| se faire avoir | *be taken for a ride, had* |
| ammocher | *dent, scrape, bruise* |
| ramasser une veste | *be refused a dance by a girl* |
| poser un lapin | *stand s.o. up* |
| se faire saquer | *get a bad mark* |
| ramasser une banane | |
| prendre une veste | |
| être recalé | *fail an exam* |

These verbs do not occur in the present because either they are assumed to have always happened in

20

the past, i.e. one does not *get* a bad mark but one *has got* a bad mark, or they still retain their dictionary meaning in the present tense, i.e. Je ramasse une banane can only mean *I am picking up a banana*.

## 6. Past

(a) **Passé Composé**. This is by far the commonest past tense in the coarse language and is formed from the past participle and the present indicative of avoir, or for reflexive and certain other verbs, être.

J'ai paumé ma bagnole.
*I've lost my car*.

(b) **Imperfect**. The imperfect tense is most commonly used in conjunction with the passé composé in the narration of past events, e.g.:

Je roulais à cent-vingt et puis schlack, je suis rentré dans une autre bagnole.

*I was doing 75 and then pow, I hit another car*.

It also occurs on its own, frequently in answers, e.g.:

Mais qu'est-ce que tu foutais là? Je me baladais.

*But what did you do there? I bummed around*.

## 7. Future

The only future tense which exists in the coarse language is the compound future formed from the present infinitive and the present indicative of aller. The literary future, usually formed from the stem and erai, eras, era, erons, erez, eront, does not really exist in conversation.

e.g.

*I'll stow my gear over there;* would be translated by Je vais foutre mes affaires là-bas; and not by Je foutrai...which would approach a bathetic reductio ad absurdum.

## 8. Subjunctive

Compared with the occurrence of the other tenses mentioned above, that of the present subjunctive is rare, and it only does so when governed by a preposition, e.g.:

Qu'il se casse ou non, je m'en fous.

*I don't give a damn if he pushes off or not.*

N.B. Using a coarse verb in any tense other than those mentioned will have distinctly comic overtones. Therefore, be prepared for peals of laughter or quizzical looks if you say something like:

Il aurait dû flotter hier.
Which is roughly equivalent to:
*Would that it had peed with rain yesterday.*

# III  INFINITIVE

**9.** As we have seen above the Coarse verb is encountered in the infinitive because of the conversational future and of defective conjugation. It has many uses outside these, and they are considered below.

**10.** The infinitive occurs with certain prepositions:

| | |
|---|---|
| Sans rigoler | *Without laughing* |
| Pour se cuiter | *To get stoned* |
| Avant de gueuler | *Before bawling* |

**11.** The infinitive is sometimes used as a deliberative noun:

Qui taper?  *Who to con?*

**12.** Certain groups of verbs govern the present infinitive:

(a) **Verbs of wishing, desire etc.; désirer, vouloir, préférer, espérer.**

Je préfère bien rigoler.

*I prefer a good laugh.*

Il espère se tirer avant midi.

*He hopes to split before noon.*

(b) **Verbs of Motion; aller, courir, descendre, montrer, rentrer, retourner, venir, revenir.**

Ils sont allés se taper une bière quelque part.

*They've gone somewhere for a drink.*

Je ne suis pas venu voir des conneries pareilles.

*I didn't come to see crap like that.*

When the idea of purpose is emphasised, this is frequently conveyed by using **pour.**

Mes parents sont rentraient pour m'engueuler.

*My parents came back to rollock me.*

(c) **Modal Verbs in -oir; devoir, falloir, pouvoir, savoir, valoir.**

Il vaut mieux les planquer.

*It'd be better to stash them.*

Il sait se débrouiller, ce mec-là.

*That guy really knows how to take care of himself.*

(d) **Verbs of Seeing, Hearing, Feeling; écouter, entendre, sentir, regarder, apercevoir, voir.**

24

Il entendait chialer quelqu'un.

*He heard somebody blubbing.*

(e) **Faire and Laisser.**

Laisse-moi roupiller, mec.

*Let me kip, man.*

These are some of the commoner constructions which govern the present infinitive. In all other cases, where they occur in speech, the coarse language follows the lead of the literary.

## IV  PARTICIPLES

**13. Present Participle**
**(a) Adjective**

When a participle describes a state or quality, it ranks as an adjective and agrees in **Gender** and **Number** with the noun or pronoun it qualifies or refers to:

Une histoire marrante.    *A funny story.*

Des types roublards.    *Some crafty blokes.*

**(b) Participle of the Verb.**

When the present participle describes an action being performed, it is a straight participle and does not inflect:

Vingt mémés, toutes gueulant et courant.

*Twenty old dears, all yelling and running.*

**(c) Gerund with en**
(i) To convey the sense of while, in the process of:

En tapant les touristes.    *While conning the tourists.*

**(ii) Consecutive with the main verb:**

"On y va," dit-il, en liquidant son dernier sandwich.

*"Let's go," he said, polishing off his last sandwich.*

(iii) As above (ii), but when the action it expresses is performed by the subject of the main verb:

Pauvre Henri! Je l'ai écrasé en sortant de chez moi.

*Poor old Henry! I ran over him as I was leaving home.*

## (d) Noun
A present participle may be used as a noun, and then it has gender and a plural in the normal way:

Les croulants.　　　*The older generation.*

## 14. Past Participle
### (a) Adjective
(i) In the same way as the present participle, the past participle may be used adjectively and then agrees in **Gender** and **Number** with its subject:

Un type barraqué.　　　*A tough looking bloke.*

Il était vachement
　　emmerdé.　　　*He was really up-tight.*

(ii) The past participle may be considered as an adjective in phrases like:

Elle était complètement crevée.

*She was completely shattered.*

Les autres étaient bourrés, mais raides!

*The others were well and truly tanked up!*

27

## (b) As a lone participle

The past participle may stand as a verb in its own right in a dependent clause:

Les flics sortis, . . .

*When the fuzz had gone, . . .*

## (c) With Avoir

(i) The passé composé of most coarse verbs is formed from the past participle of the verb with the present indicative of avoir. In this case the participle agrees with its **preceding direct object:**

Je les ai tous emmerdés.

*I got them all up-tight.*

Il m'a embrassée sur le cou.
*He kissed me on the neck.*

(ii) Where the object does not precede, or there is no object, there is no agreement:

Ils ont pris une belle cuite.

*They got really well smashed.*

(iii) The past participles of impersonal verbs, and of **faire** when it governs another verb are invariable:

Il nous a fait casquer pour lui.

*He made us cough up for him.*

## (d) Reflexive Verbs.

The past participle of reflexive verbs, although

formed with **être,** follows the rule for agreement of **avoir.**

(i) Usually the reflexive pronoun is itself the preceding direct object and there is consequently agreement:

Elle s'est tapé tout son boulot.

*She finished off all her work.*

(ii) Occasionally the reflexive pronoun is **dative** and then there is no agreement:

Il nous a payé un verre.

*He bought us a drink.*

(e) **Noun.**

The past participle may be used, like the present participle, as a noun:

| | |
|---|---|
| Un décontracté | *A cool guy* |
| Un empaffé | *A queer* |

# V SUBJUNCTIVE

**15.** As mentioned before in Section II, the subjunctive mood is relatively rare in the Coarse Language, and only occurs when governed by a preposition. In general then, it is wise to treat the subjunctive of coarse verbs with extreme caution, unless you are deliberately trying to be funny.

However, the straight verbs that occur in speech, and there are, of necessity, many of them, are more likely to be used in the subjunctive, although by no means frequently. When they are used, they follow the rules of literary French.

It may be useful to point out where the Coarse Language would drop a subjunctive for an indicative:

The stylistically correct:

Il semble qu'il soit paumé.

*It seems that he's lost.*

is much more likely to occur conversationally as:

Il semble qu'il est paumé.

# VI GENDER OF NOUNS

**16.** As in straight French, all coarse nouns have a gender and a number, and the choice of which gender, except for nouns of obvious sex, is quite as arbitrary as in the literary language.

As you might expect,

une nana                *a girl, chick, bird*

is feminine and

un mec                  *a bloke*

is masculine.

However, I list below some of the coarse nouns which are quite common, and are of a different gender than one might expect:

un boudin
un dauphin              *fat girl, boot*

un cachalot
un cageot               *scrawny bird*

un tas de tôle          *slag-heap, tarty chick*

and here are some very coarse nouns, which seem to be, logically speaking, of entirely the wrong gender:

le con
le barbu                *female genitalia*

31

la queue
la bite
la pine
la balayette          *virile member*

les joyeuses          *testes*

Apart from these more obvious anomalies, the coarse noun is subject to just the same somewhat twisted Logic of Gender of the literary language.

# VII FEMININE OF NOUNS AND ADJECTIVES

**17.** A certain number of coarse nouns describing living beings may have a masculine and a feminine form for the different sexes.

Similarly, coarse adjectives have two forms, as you would expect, and where agreement is necessary they agree.

(a) In the simplest case, the feminine form is distinguished by a final **e** added to the masculine stem:

| | |
|---|---|
| une flemmarde | *a lazy chick* |
| une trouillarde | *a female coward* |

(b) Where the noun or adjective in question already has a final **e**, it remains unchanged in the feminine and only the article changes:

| | |
|---|---|
| une môme | |
| une gosse | |
| une mioche | *female kid, nipper* |
| une dégueulasse | *bitch* |
| une morphale | *gutsy female* |

(c) There are, however, certain variations. Below I list some of the commoner distinct feminine forms that occur:

33

| un salaud | une salope |
|-----------|-----------|
| *bastard, swine* | *bitch* |
| un con | une conasse |
| *dozy sod* | *dozy old boot* |
| un copain | une copine |
| *mate, pal* | *female friend* |
| un greluchon | une greluche |
| *dozy bloke* | *dozy chick* |
| un emmerdeur | une emmerdeuse |
| *pain in the ass* | *ditto* |
| un dingo | une dingote |
| *nutter* | *ditto* |

(d) Adjectives and participles used as nouns have a feminine form where necessary, and this is usually formed by adding a final -e:

une paumée          *a disconcerted chick*

When the addition of an extra -e is impossible due to the prior presence of a final -e, the word is invariable and only the article changes:

une myope          *a short-sighted girl*

(e) Occasionally it is necessary to double the consonant which will precede the final -e of an adjective or adjective used as a noun:

une mignonne
une minette          *a tasty piece*

34

# VIII PLURAL OF NOUNS AND ADJECTIVES

**18.** All coarse nouns and adjectives have a plural form, where a plural is possible.

(a) This is usually formed by adding a final -s:

| | |
|---|---|
| un mec | trois mecs |
| *a bloke* | *three blokes* |
| un flic | les flics |
| *a copper* | *the fuzz* |
| une nana | des nanas |
| *a chick* | *some chicks* |

(b) Certain of them add a final -x to make the plural:

| | |
|---|---|
| un pieu | sept pieux |
| *a bed* | *seven beds* |

(c) No change occurs in the plural if the noun or adjective ends with an -s, -x, -z:

| | |
|---|---|
| un type schlass | tous les types schlass |
| *one stoned guy* | *all the stoned guys* |

(d) Singular in *–au, eau, eu,* plural in *–aux, –eaux, –eux:*

| | |
|---|---|
| un noyeau | ses noyeaux |
| *a nut* | *his nuts* |

| un tuyau | mille tuyaux |
| *tip* | *a thousand tips* |

(e) Singular in *–al*, plural in *–aux*:*

| un cheval | mes chevaux |
| *a horse* | *my horses* |

## 19. Compound Nouns

(a) Only such parts of a compound noun as are themselves nouns or adjectives can have a plural form. Elements which are adverbs, verbs, or prepositions are invariable:

| une chauffe-cul | les chauffe-culs de Paris |
| *a P.T.* | *the P.T.s of Paris* |

(b) Where there are two nouns in a compound, and one remains singular in meaning in the plural, then only the other takes a plural ending:

| une armoire-à-glace | les armoires-à-glace |
| *a thug* | *the thugs* |

*Some words in —al, have a plural in —als, e.g. un futal, des futals

# IX POSITION AND AGREEMENT OF ADJECTIVES

**20.** Basically the rules for positioning adjectives are absolutely the same for the coarse as well as the literary language, and this is the case as regards agreement.

However, those who speak coarse French are much less pedantic about such things, and as long as the meaning is quite clear they are not bothered about the niceties of literary style.

I will summarise very briefly the 3 main points which refer to these topics:

(i) Adjectives agree in **Gender** and **Number** with the noun which they qualify or refer to:

une grammaire chiante
*a draggy old grammar book*

(ii) In the vast majority of cases the adjective follows the noun to which it refers. This is not the case for certain very common adjectives, which normally precede the noun upon which they depend. Here are some of the most important:

| | |
|---|---|
| bon (meilleur) | méchant |
| court | jeune |
| joli | mauvais (pire) |
| long | vaste |

37

| | |
|---|---|
| petit (moindre) | pauvre* |
| grand* | vilain |
| haut | vieux |
| gros | |

(iii) If a noun is qualified by an **adverb** or **phrase** the adjective, including those in (ii), follows its noun:

une mémé vachement grosse
*a very fat old bag*

## 21. No Agreement

It is a feature of the Coarse Language that there are certain adjectives that occur in it which do not agree with the noun they qualify. This may be partly because the feminine forms have unpleasant assonances, but more likely because the speaker is, albeit unwittingly, thumbing his nose at the grammarians. I list below some of the most common examples:

| | |
|---|---|
| paf | *tight, whistled* |
| sympa' | *nice, pleasant* |
| rigolo | *good for a laugh* |
| con | *stupid, boring* |

*There are a certain number of adjectives which occur in French that have a different meaning if they precede, or if they follow the noun they refer to. Some of the more frequent are listed below:

|         | Preceding | Following |
|---------|-----------|-----------|
| grand   | *distinguished* | *tall* |
| pauvre  | *unlucky* | *poor* |
| sale    | *bloody* | *dirty* |
| seul    | *single (only one)* | *alone* |
| prochain | *next* | *subsequent* |
| propre  | *own* | *clean* |
| vrai    | *true (=good)* | *true (=genuine)* |
| nouveau | *new (=fresh)* | *new (=novel)* |
| dernier | *last (of several)* | *last (preceding)* |
| cher    | *dear (as a friend)* | *expensive* |
| brave   | *fine, good* | *valiant* |

# X ADVERBS

**22. Formation**

**(a) Regular**

The vast majority of adverbs are formed by adding -ment to the **feminine form** of the adjective:

(i) Adjectives ending in a **consonant**:

sensationnel            sensationnellement
*groovy*

(ii) Adjectives which have a masculine form ending in -e, and hence no change in the feminine:

vache            vachement
*nasty, unpleasant* **but**   *very*

(iii) Adjectives with a **different** feminine form, **fou: folle**

follement
*madly*

**(b)** (i) -ment is added to the **masculine** form of certain adjectives which end in a vowel:

vrai            vraiment
*true*            *truly, really*

(ii) A few adjectives also add a **circumflex** to the

final consonant of the masculine form, before adding the adverbial flexion:

| | |
|---|---|
| assidu | assidûment |
| *diligent* | *diligently* |

(c) Adjectives with present participal endings, i.e. -ent, -ant form adverbs thus:

| | |
|---|---|
| marrant | marramment |
| *funny (ha ha)* | *funnily* |

(d) Certain adjectives change the final -e of the feminine form to -é before taking the adverbial flexion:

| | |
|---|---|
| profond | profondément |
| *deep* | *deeply* |

(e) A small group of adjectives with a masculine form ending in -e behave similarly:

| | |
|---|---|
| énorme | énormément |
| *enormous* | *enormously* |

**23.** There are certain coarse adjectives which do not readily take an adverbial flexion, such as:

| | |
|---|---|
| chiant | *draggy* |
| rigolo | *good for a laugh* |
| pénard | *cushy, easy* |
| dingue | *mad, crazy* |

41

| cucu | *pansy, affected* |
| con | *stupid, boring* |
| crado(ck) | *dirty, shabby* |

Adverbial senses for these words are best conveyed by a phrase, or some other method, e.g.:

| avec un accent cucu | *with a fairy voice* |

## 24. Vachement

This adverb, which appeared as an example in 22 (ii), and which is equivalent to the literary French **très** in almost every way, is by far the commonest coarse adverb. As such it provides a useful marker for the Coarse Language, since it does not exist at all in correct French. Therefore, anyone using this adverb will inevitably be using other slang as well, and will not be wildly surprised if you do too. Along with the verb **foutre,** used in its slang connotations and the adjective **dégueulasse, vachement** forms a trio of signal words which give the surest indication of opportunities to exercise one's fluency in the Coarse Language.

# XI  POSITIONING OF ADVERBS

Usage regarding the positioning of adverbs is not at all fixed, and depends quite often on conditions of balance and emphasis.

**25.** As a general rule, the adverb *follows* the verb that it qualifies:

Je bosse de préférence le soir.

*I prefer to gnome in the evenings.*

**26.** When an adverb qualifies a verb in a **compound tense** or **infinitive.**

(i) Adverbs of Time; **aussitôt, hier, demain, aujourd'-hui, plus tôt** *follow* the infinitive or past tense; as do those of Place:

Tu l'as foutu là.          *You heaved it there.*

Il s'est cassé hier.       *He hit the road yesterday.*

(ii) Long or cumbersome adverbs, together with most adverbial phrases *follow* the past participle or infinitive:

Je ne peux pas bouquiner longtemps.

*I can't read for long.*

43

Il l'a fait sans faire d'histoires.

*He did it without turning a hair.*

(iii) Short adverbs, plus a few short adverbial phrases *precede* the past participle or infinitive:

Tu aurais bien pu me filer du fric.

*You could have easily lent me some bread.*

**27.** If an adverb qualifies another adverb, or a participle, adjective, or adverbial expression, it normally precedes it:

Elle est extrêmement moche.

*She's as ugly as sin.*

Un type bien fringué.

*A well dressed guy.*

**28.** Adverbs and adverbial expressions which link a sentence with something that has gone before it usually start the sentence:

Là-bas ils cassaient la gueule d'un prof' de maths.

*Over there a maths master was getting his lumps.*

**29.** In a case where emphasis is required, the adverb may be placed at the beginning of the sentence:

Tant elle était moche...

*She was so ugly...*

**30.** Adverbs which qualify a whole sentence or idea may be placed anywhere but occur most frequently at the start of the sentence:

Mais sans blague, je n'en sais rien.

*Straight up, I don't know anything.*

**31.** Adverbs which qualify a Numeral or an Indefinite Adjective follow the word in question:

Pour mille balles seulement.

*For a lousy quid.*

# XII COMPARISON

**32.** Formation of the Comparative and Superlative of Adjectives

(a)

|  | Positive | Comparative | Superlative |
|---|---|---|---|
| **Mas. Sing.** | con | plus con | le plus con |
|  | *stupid* | *more stupid* | *the stupidest* |
| **Fem. Sing.** | mignonne | plus mignonne | la plus mignonne |
|  | *tasty* | *tastier* | *the tastiest* |
| **Mas. Plur.** | chiants | plus chiants | les plus chiants |
|  | *draggy* | *draggier* | *the draggiest* |
| **Fem. Plur.** | paumées | plus paumées | les plus paumées |
|  | *lost* | *more lost* | *the most lost* |

(b) **Moins** is used in exactly the same way to decrease the degree of the adjective:

| moins pénard | *less cushy* |
|---|---|
| la moins salope | *the least bitchy* |

**33. Usage**

(a) Comparative and Superlative forms may stand before or after the noun they qualify as usage or emphasis demands:

Une plus chiante mémé   *A draggier old dear*

Des bagnoles plus rapides *Faster cars*

(b) When a superlative follows a noun both articles remain:

La boîte la plus terrible   *The grooviest club*

(c) If a superlative is preceded by a **Possessive Adjective,** the Definite Article is omitted, *unless* the superlative **follows** the noun:

Mes plus chics copains   *My smoothest mates*

Ma copine la plus sexy   *My sexiest chick*

(d) Similarly the Definite Article is omitted after **de** in expressions such as **ce qu'il y a de:**

Ce qu'il y a de moins barbant
*Whatever is the least boring*

(e) Comparatives and Superlatives are used with **de:**

C'est le plus con du quartier
*He's the thickest round here*

However **de** is omitted after **beaucoup:**

47

Elle est beaucoup plus mignonne

*She's much tastier*

### 34. Comparative and Superlative of the Adverb

These are formed in exactly the same way as those of adjectives, **but** the **le** added in the Superlative is **invariable**:

Cette nana marche le moins joliement.

*That chick walks the least prettily.*

### 35. If two superlatives qualify the same noun the Definite Article is repeated:

La bagnole la plus dégueulasse et la plus ammochée.

*The most disgusting and the most beaten up car.*

### 36. Plus, Davantage, Moins

Where **plus** conveys the idea of more it is followed by **de**:

Henri a plus de fric que moi.
*Henri has more bread than I have.*

The same is true of **moins** used to convey the opposite.

**Davantage** can be used similarly:

Il demande davantage de pognon.
*He wants more bread.*

48

### 37. Genuine or false Comparisons

(a) When expressing **more than, less than** as a genuine comparison **que** is used:

Ce couillon-là est vachement plus salaud que moi.

*That s.o.b. is much more of a bastard than I am.*

(b) When **more than, less than** express a more concrete idea, i.e. a quantity greater (or less) than, **de** is used:

Louis demandait plus de vingt mille balles.

*Louis asked for more than twenty quid.*

### 38. Don't forget the French negated comparison, where the **ne** has no negative force:

Il est plus calé que tu ne penses.

*He's more of a gnome than you think.*

### 39. In literary French, though very rarely in conversation, inversion is common if the subject of the subordinate clause is a noun:

Ce boulot est moins pénard que ne pensent mes copains.

*This job is less cushy than my mates think.*

### 40. However, if the main clause is negated the second **ne** is omitted:

Pom-Pom n'est pas si dingue que tu crois.

*Pompidou isn't as thick as you think.*

## 41. De plus en plus, de moins en moins

The adjective follows the phrase and agrees in Gender and Number with its subject:

La grammaire qui devient de moins en moins marrante.

*The grammar that gets less and less funny.*

# XIII  INTERROGATIVES

## 42. Conversation

The literary French **n'est-ce pas** has fallen into abeyance in the Coarse Language and has been replaced by two single words: **hein** and **quoi.**

They are substituted for the literary construction and are used in exactly the same way. However, **hein** has the overtones of the English **eh,** and is consequently somewhat inelegant, also it is the sort of thing young Frogs are told not to say at school. This makes it less acceptable than **quoi.**

I like to think that there is something of the English interrogative *what* embodied in the French, as typified by phrases like:

*Wizard prang, what?*

However this is quite beside the point.
**Quoi** is used in the following way:

C'était vachement bon, quoi?

*Bloody good, wasn't it?*

**43.** There are certain features of the Coarse Language, when it is spoken, as it invariably is (see Introduction), which differ from the written. The usual interrogative constructions of **Inversion** and **Est-ce que** are largely defunct. A question is usually posed by intonation, rather than by rearrangement of the elements of the sentence. Thus, you would say:

Tu me files un clope?    *Give us a fag.*

rather than

Me files-tu un clope?

which, in fact, would sound pompous and bathetic, and which is now redundant with demands of this nature.


**44.** **Inversion** is occasionally used to emphasise the interrogative nature of a demand, and is frequently associated with repetition of the subject:

Jean, as-tu bouffé ou non?

*John, have you eaten or not?*

**N.B.** It is as well to remember that polite conversation still demands the literary forms and Officialese abounds with them. They are merely much less frequent in Coarse Speech. You run the risk of shocking people if you use coarse forms indiscriminately, and let us not forget there are always fifty Frogs on hand to correct ones French at the slightest provocation.

## 45. Interrogative Words Introducing a Direct Question
(a) **Qui, quel, lequel**

When one of these words introduces a question as subject or complement, it precedes the verb. **Lequel** and its inflected forms as objects of the sentence tend to cause inversion.

Qui a chipé mes godasses, hein?
*Who's pinched my shoes, eh?*

Laquelle veux-tu draguer?
*Which one do you fancy?*

(b) Inversion occurs when a question is prefixed by **que**:

Que veux-tu?                *What do you want?*

## 46. If the subject of the question is a Personal Pronoun or **on** or **ce** simple inversion occurs:

A quoi penses-tu?        *What are you thinking?*

Pourquoi ne sort-on pas?
*Why don't we go out somewhere?*

53

### 47. Complex Inversion
(a) This occurs after **pourquoi** if the subject is a noun:

Pourquoi ce mec ne fout-il pas le camp?

*Why doesn't this bloke push off?*

(b) or if the verb has an object other than a reflexive pronoun:

Comment ce type va-t-il payer sa claque?

*How's this bloke going to pay his round?*


### 48.
If longer Interrogative Pronouns are used (**qu'est-ce que** etc.) the order is that of a simple statement:

Qu'est-ce que t'as foutu aujourd'hui?

*What have you been doing today, mate?*


### 49. Indirect Questions
There is no inversion if an indirect question is introduced by an interrogative word; **si, qui, que** etc.:

Serge demandait si je voulais sortir avec lui.

*Serge asked if I wanted to go out with him.*


### 50. Other Interrogative Statements
(a) Short phrases can be used to involve the person

addressed in your train of thought, or to ask their opinion without formulating a proper question:

J'aime bien danser le jerk. Et toi?

*I like dancing. How about you?*

(b) **Tu sais, vous savez**

These phrases can be tacked on to any statement, just like the colloquial English *you know* to add colour or emphasis to your conversation:

Ce type est vachement marrant, tu sais.

*He's a damn funny chap, you know.*

Strictly speaking, however, they are not questions but pure rhetorical adjuncts.

### 51. Answers

(a) There are three basic one word answers; **oui**, **non** and **si** (if yes has a contradictory sense). They are used quite straightforwardly:

Tu sors ce soir? Non.
*Are you going out tonight? No.*

T'as pas vu mon froc? Si, dans l'armoire.

*You haven't seen my trousers, have you? Yes, in the wardrobe.*

(b) It is rare in both the coarse and polite languages to hear **oui** or **non** on their own. They tend to be reinforced by another word or phrase:

| Mais oui! | *Oh yes!* |
| Pas du tout! | *Not at all!* |
| Mais si! | *Yes (it is)!* |
| Absolument pas | *Definitely not!* |
| Mais non! | *Not at all!* |
| Oui, vachement! | *Yes, very!* |

**52.** Frogs do not use *merci*, except as a polite negative, e.g.:

Tu veux un clope?    *Do you want a fag?*

Non, merci (or simply merci).    *No thanks.*

If you wish to reply in the affirmative, you must use the phrase *je veux bien*. Like merci it may occur on its own, or with a single word answer, in this case oui:

Tu veux qu'on se tape une bière?
Oui, je veux bien.

*Would you like to come for a drink?*
*Sure.*

**53. D'accord** (or sometimes d'acc)
This may be used as a simple affirmative, instead of je veux bien, for informal replies. It has a similar force to the English *fair enough*, or *O.K.* (which does also occur in French):

On va rien foutre cet après-midi.* D'accord.

*Let's do sweet F.A. this afternoon. Fair enough.*


## 54. Disarming Answers and Crushers

A questioner may be disconcerted and politely informed that you are not interested in what he is saying, or that you do not really believe what he has said, by using the phrases:

| | |
|---|---|
| **Tiens donc!** | **Ah bon!** |
| **Dis donc!** | **Sans blague!** |

e.g.

Je suis membre de l'équipage d'Apollo 11.

Tiens donc!

*I am a crew member of Apollo 11.*

*You don't say.*


**55.** The sentiment of the English phrase: *you must be joking* is best conveyed in French by one of the phrases:

| | |
|---|---|
| **Tu parles!** | **Tu veux rire!** |
| **Tu rigoles!** | **Mon oeil!** |

---

* You will have noticed elsewhere the use of an impersonal construction with **on** in informal proposals of this sort. This is a common coarse form of rendering the English *Let's* plus an infinitive.

e.g.

Puis-je prendre la bagnole ce soir, papa ?*

Tu parles!

*May I borrow the car tonight, dad?*

*Like hell you can!*

### 56. Note on Pronunciation

Young Frogs, and especially in Paris (les parigots), pronounce the formal French **oui** as **ouais** or **hui** and both these forms are quite acceptable in coarse conversation. However, in polite conversation, they may well cause adverse comment, especially **ouais.**

### 57. Ben

This word is derived from the polite **eh bien** (*well . . .*) and corresponds nicely to the English *er*, *well*, *um. . . .* Consequently, it is a splendid hiatus filler.

If someone turns to you at a Froggy cocktail-party, and asks your opinion on (say) Early Etruscan Nose-fluting, you may cover your embarrassment, and/or your lack of knowledge, by saying reflectively **ben** and, perhaps adding some other stock hiatus-filling phrases.

This reply will establish that you have understood the question, and thereby spare you its repetition,

* Please note the polite inversion necessitated by important demands of this sort.

which would doubtless be executed as if you were both mentally deficient and very deaf. Furthermore, if you are able to spin out this gambit long enough, your assaillant will probably set off on a long and shatteringly boring monologue, which is what he wanted to do anyway, and you are spared having to answer at all.

## 58. Hiatus-Filling Phrases

| | |
|---|---|
| C'est à dire | *I mean to say* |
| Tu sais | |
| Vous savez | *You know* |

C'est une question bien difficile
*That's a tough nut to crack*

# XV  NEGATION

**59.**

(a) **Non** is used for direct negative answers (**51**).

(b) In coarse speech **pas** is frequently found on its own:

| | |
|---|---|
| Pas un rond | *Not a penny* |
| Pas vrai | *You don't say* |

## 60. Negative Forms
Ne pas

Although literary usage demands that verbs are negated by a pair such as: **ne pas**, it is not infrequent to find the **ne** omitted in speech, having been, often elided out of the sentence, e.g.:

T'as pas vu mes tatanes?
*Have you seen my shoes?*

Il voulait pas sortir.
*He didn't want to go out.*

**61.** The **ne** of other negative pairs may be omitted in this way in speech. The principal pairs are:

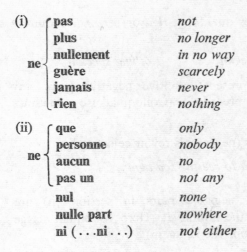

(i)
| ne | pas | *not* |
| | plus | *no longer* |
| | nullement | *in no way* |
| | guère | *scarcely* |
| | jamais | *never* |
| | rien | *nothing* |

(ii)
| ne | que | *only* |
| | personne | *nobody* |
| | aucun | *no* |
| | pas un | *not any* |
| | nul | *none* |
| | nulle part | *nowhere* |
| | ni ( . . .ni . . .) | *not either* |

e.g.

Je veux plus gaspiller mon temps avec cette con de grammaire.

*I don't want waste any more time on this bloody grammar.*

Personne était là.

*There was no-one there.*

(a) **Non plus** occurs occasionally to add emphasis to a negative pair. If it does so, the **ne** frequently remains and the **pas** is omitted:

Je ne trichais non plus.

*I wasn't cheating either.*

61

(b) Adjectives qualifying **rien** or **personne** require a preceding **de**:

Rien de spécial.  *Nothing special.*

(c) With a present infinitive negative pairs stay together and precede it. (Colloquial use sometimes drops the **ne**):

Je préfèrais (ne) jamais revoir ce conard.

*I never want to see the sod again.*

(d) However, negative pairs in section (ii) are separated by the infinitive: (Here colloquial usage sometimes drops the **ne** again)

Il (ne) voulait voir personne.

*He didn't want to see anyone.*


**62.** In a double negative **ne** disappears:

e.g. **Plus personne**

Après minuit il y a plus personne.

*There's nobody after midnight.*


**63. Pas** is omitted in certain set locutions:

N'importe.  *It doesn't matter.*


Here endeth the sections on grammar. Now on to the vocabulary lists we've all be waiting for.

# Vocabulary Lists

## I  USEFUL PHRASES

Perhaps the best way, and certainly the easiest, of loosening up ones literary French is to use some of the stock idiomatic phrases which abound in the Coarse Language. I list some of them below. They are many and various, but these are some of the basic ones. I shall also try to indicate some aspects of their usage and any dangers of making embarrassing howlers.

**Ça y est**: is used to denote sufficiency and may be translated by "*that's it*" or "*that's enough*".

e.g.

Recule un peu.

*Back up a bit.*

Ça y est.

*That's it.*

**et ta soeur**?: This little gem wraps up in three short words the phrase "*and the same to you, mate!*". It

63

is an answer for virtually any insult or cutting remark, and places the ball smartly in your assaillants court, whether or not his parents had any female issue. It is, after all a purely rhetorical question (ho ho).

e.g.

Vas te faire foutre!
*Get stuffed!*

Et ta soeur?
*And the same to you!*

**et ainsi?**   Irony here with some of the equivalents of

**et alors?**   "big deal", "so what" etc.

e.g.

Hé toi, t'as pris ma place!

*Hey, that's my seat!*

Et ainsi?
*So what?\**

A more picturesque way of expressing the "*big deal*" idea is to use the phrase:

**Ça me fait une belle jambe.**

---

\*I advise people of slight build under five foot nine to exercise a certain amount of caution with these two phrases. Frogs do get awfully stroppy if you put them down.

Beautiful legs apart, this phrase is conjugated for use in conversation, thus:

Ça lui faisait une belle jambe.

Ça te fera une belle jambe

However, the rules of section **2** still apply and you must beware of comic reductio ad absurdum, such as:

Ça a fallu nous faire une belle jambe.

The meaning of which is certainly obscure.
The phrase is used as follows:

Ça te fera une belle jambe, mon vieux. Il s'est tiré.

*There's no point, old son. He's pushed off.*

**je me casse les pieds:** This is a simple and useful phrase and expresses a feeling of boredom.

e.g.
Salut Georges, ça va?

*Hi George, how are you?*

Non, je me casse les pieds ici.

*I'm bored out of my mind.*

## II  HANDY ADJECTIVES AND ADVERBS

Here are some useful current adjectives and adverbs, which are not to be found in the average glossary. I shall indicate any cause for care as necessary.

**dégueulasse**        *disgusting, nasty*

e.g.

Les bars à Acton sont dégueulasses.
*The bars in Acton are revolting.*

**dégueu'**    a more acceptable form of the above

**cuit**
**bourré**
**paf**
**rond**
**schlass**     *drunk, smashed, knotted*

e.g.

Merde alors, comme il était bourré.

*Bloody Hell, he really was stoned.*

**N.B.** Schlass is extremely coarse and should be used with caution.

**con**     *stupid, idiotic, useless*

This is a general term of near abuse and conveys disapproval of many kinds.

66

e.g.

Le film était vachement con.

*It was a bloody awful film.*

**con comme un balai** *very stupid (only of people)*

**calé** *bright, clever, hard-working*

**balèse** *smooth, fly (school slang)*

**sympa'** *nice, plesant*
*(usually of people)*

**marrant** *funny (ha ha)*

e.g.

C'est un type marrant.

*He's an amusing bloke.*

**rigolo** *good for a laugh*
*(often ironic)*

e.g.

Ce n'est pas tres rigolo.

*That's not much fun*

**pénard** *cushy, easy*
*(of a job especially)*

**mignon\*** *sweet, pretty, good-looking*

\*This is definitely a positive adjective, when applied to girls, but is pejorative for men, suggesting effeminacy.

**paumé**               *lost (physically), (fig)*
                        *disconcerted*

e.g.

Le pauvre type était complètement paumé.

*The poor sod was way out of his depth.*

**rapé**
**foutu**
**baisé**               *screwed-up, non-functional*

This may only be applied to inanimate objects with this meaning. The last two when applied to people have quite a different meaning!

e.g.

Ma bagnole est complètement foutue.
*My car is well and truly buggered.*

**dingue**              *mad, crazy, nutty (of people)*

**moche**               *ugly, unattractive*

e.g.

C'était une histoire moche.

*It was a nasty story.*

**crevé**
**cané**
**vané**                *tired, shattered, shagged out*

**cucu**                *pansy, affected*

This is particularly used when describing affectations of style or dress.

| | |
|---|---|
| **de la foutaise** | |
| **du balai** | |
| **du bidon** | *rubbish, nonsense, balls* |

These phrases may be used as interjections or in complete sentences.

e.g.

Tout ça c'est de la foutaise.

*That's a lot of bullshit.*

| | |
|---|---|
| **fauché** | |
| **raide** | *skint, broke* |
| **crado(ck)** | *dirty, tatty, run down* |
| **chiant** | *draggy, a drag* |

e.g.

C'est un mec chiant.

*He's a drag.*

| | |
|---|---|
| **décontracté** | *cool, smooth (usually of people)* |
| **roublard** | *scheming, sneaky, fly* |
| **du toc** | |
| **de la camelotte** | *cheap, tatty, crappy (especially of clothes)* |

I list below some of the trendier ways of expressing approval. They change from week to week, and vary

69

from one group of people to another. Once they are out of fashion they are quite often used ironically, like the English "with it" for example.

**terrible**
**chouette**
**le pied**

**dément (ciel)**
**sensationnel** (sometimes occurs as **sensass**)

e.g.
J'ai trouvé une boîte terrible à Paris.

*I've found this great club in Paris.*

## III SOME COMMON NOUNS

You will find in this list some very current words which either are not to be found in normal vocabularies, or which have a coarse meaning beyond the scope of most glossaries.

**une nana**
**une pépé**        *girl, bird, chick*

These words are usually complementary, expressing mild approbation. Pejorative words of this type may be found in Appendix 3 on Abuse. This is also the case with the nouns referring to males.

e.g.
Elle était une vraie petite nana.

*She was a tasty little piece.*

**un mec**
**un type**        *bloke, chap, guy*
**un gars**        *bloke (with beery overtones)*

e.g.
Je prenais un pot avec les gars.

*I was having a jar with the lads.*

**une mémé**        *grandma'; old dear*

e.g.

Attention mémé!

*Watch out, love!*

| | |
|---|---|
| **un pépé** | *grandad, old codger* |
| **un copain** | *friend, mate, pal* |
| **une copine** | *female friend (as opposed to girl friend)* |

To convey the English idea of *girl-friend*, you must use a possessive adjective:

e.g.

**ma copine**

*my girl-friend*

or use a different term, such as:

**une girl-friend**
**une petite amie**

e.g.

Où est ta petite amie?

*Where's your chick?*

| | |
|---|---|
| **la flotte** | |
| **la baille** | *water* |

e.g.

Ploof! il tombait dans la flotte.

*Splash! he fell into the drink.*

| un dingo | nutter, idiot (not necessarily |
| une dingote | pejorative) |

| une baffe | clout, clip (used familiarily |
| | only) |

| un truc | |
| un machin | thing, thingumyjig |

| le fric | |
| le pognon | |
| le pèse | |
| les ronds | |
| les sous | money, bread |

| un balle | I old franc |

The word *balle* is seldom used in figures below a thousand. Also the phrase *mille balles* approximates in many ways to the English *quid*.

e.g.

**cinq mille balles**
*five quid (not a direct monetary equivalence, of course)*

| un ticket | mille balles |
| un sac | dix mille balles |
| une connerie | an action which is silly or useless |

e.g.

Cesse tes conneries!

*Stop sodding about!*

73

| une piaule | room, pad |
|---|---|

| un paddock | |
|---|---|
| un pucier | |
| un pieu | bed, sack (*literal and sexual*) |

e.g.

Je veux aller au paddock
*I want to hit the hay.*

| la boufftance | food, nosh |
|---|---|

| la trouille | |
|---|---|
| le trac | fear, butterflies |

e.g.

J'avais le trac

*I was scared*

| un trouillard | coward, gutless wonder |
|---|---|

| un métèque | foreigner |
|---|---|

| un gosse | |
|---|---|
| un môme | |
| un mioche | kid, nipper |

| un plouc | |
|---|---|
| un moujik | bumpkin, country lad, peasant |

These words are frequently used pejoratively by townspeople to describe clumsy or unsophisticated people. *Plouc* may also be used as an adjective in this context.

| un bazar(d) | *mess* |

e.g.
Quel bazar!
*What a mess!*

| un bringueur | *smoothie, playboy, lad* |
| décontraction | *cool, presence of mind* |

## IV. USEFUL VERBS

**se cuiter**
**prendre une cuite**    *get drunk, smashed*

**avoir la gueule de bois**    *be hung over*

**claquer tr.**

**casquer intr.**    *pay out, cough up money*

The different uses may be shown by:

J'ai claqué quinze mille balles.

*I coughed up fifteen quid.*

Il a fallu casquer pour lui.

*I had to pay for him.*

**se magner le cul**    *hurry up, move over or up*

e.g.

Magnes ton cul!

*Budge over!* or *Shift your butt!*

**avoir la trouille**
  **le trac**    *be scared, shit scared*

**foutre la trouille**    *scare, terrify*

**se taper**    *go and get; polish off*

e.g.

| | |
|---|---|
| se taper une bière | *go for a drink* |
| se taper le boulot | *polish off ones work* |

| | |
|---|---|
| se balader | |
| trainer | *wander about, tool around* |

e.g.

Je me suis baladé toute la nuit à Montmartre.
*I tooled around Montmartre all night*

| | |
|---|---|
| taper | *cadge, con, sponge* |

e.g.

Je l'ai tapé pour un clope.

*I cadged a fag from him.*

| | |
|---|---|
| planquer | *hide, stash* |
| bouffer | |
| grailler | *eat, nosh* |

These verbs give rise to such expressions as:

**à la bouffe**
**graille**

which mean that food is ready or that *grub is up*.

| | |
|---|---|
| liquider | *polish off; bump off* |
| rigoler | |
| se marrer | *laugh, have a good time* |

e.g.

On a bien rigolé chez Franck hier soir.

*We had a good time at Frank's last night.*

| | |
|---|---|
| **paumer** | *lose tr.* |
| giving rise to: | |
| **se paumer** | *to lose ones way* |
| **rouler** | *con, take s.o. for a ride* |
| **flotter** | |
| **chaggater** | *piss with rain* |
| **bêcher** | *cut s.o. dead* |
| **roupiller** | *sleep, kip* |
| **se tirer** | |
| **se casser** | |
| **se barrer** | *leave, split, push off* |

e.g.

On se tire?
*Let's split.*

| | |
|---|---|
| **gueuler** | *shout, scream* |
| **engueuler** | *nag, rollock, dress down* |
| **plaquer** | |
| **larguer** | *give s.t. up, jack in* |

78

e.g.

J'ai plaqué philo'.
*I've given up philosophy.*

Je l'ai largué comme une vieille chaussette.
*I jacked her in like an old boot.*

**s'en foutre**     *not to give a damn*

e.g.

Je m'en fous pas mal.

*I don't give a damn.*

**en avoir marre de**
**en avoir sa claque**
**en avoir ras le bol**     *to have had enough, a gutful of*

e.g.

J'en ai marre de tes salades.
*I've had just about enough of your sodding about.*

**emmerder**     *annoy, hack off, be a drag*

e.g.

Tu m'emmerdes.

*You're a drag.*

**s'emmerder**     *to be bored to death, fed up*

**louper**     *miss*

e.g.

J'ai loupé le train.
*I missed the train.*

79

| | |
|---|---|
| **se faire avoir** | *to be had, taken for a ride* |
| **ammocher** | *dent, scrape, bruise* |

e.g.

Louis a ammoché sa bagnole.

*Louis has pranged his car.*

| | |
|---|---|
| **piquer** | |
| **chiper** | *pinch, nick, lift* |
| **se casser la tête** | *worry, be worried, sweat about s.t.* |

e.g.

(Te) casse pas la tête!

*Don't get your knickers in a twist!*

| | |
|---|---|
| **chialer** | *cry, blub* |
| **foutre le bazar** | *mess up, make a mess* |

## V CLOTHES AND CLOTHING

| | |
|---|---|
| une liquette<br>une limace | *shirt* |
| un futal<br>un froc<br>un falzar<br>un bénard | *pair of trousers* |
| les godasses<br>les tatanes<br>les pompes<br>les grolles | *pair of shoes* |
| un costard | *suit* |
| les fringues<br>les nippes | *clothes, gear* |
| bien fringué<br>nippé<br>sapé | *well-dressed, smart* |
| avoir la sape | *be well dressed* |
| être en bleu | *be in working gear* |
| avoir de la gueule | *be in fashion, impressive* |
| être en dégueulasse | *be sloppily, casually dressed* |

# Appendices

## I DANS UNE BOITE QUELCONQUE

Imagine, if you will, the scene in a Froggy discothèque. The room is packed with couples and single people all grooving to the latest transatlantic sounds. The air is filled with the smoke of English and American cigarettes. There is a heady scent of warm flesh and the inevitable "whisky coca". Some greasy Frog has asked you for the upteenth time if you want a drink. At twenty francs a go he must be joking. Politely, but firmly, you have told him to go and get stuffed. While he is looking for the Heavy Mob you are listening to the conversations around you. Here are some of the words and phrases you are bound to hear:

| | |
|---|---|
| **une boîte (de nuit)** | *night club, discothèque* |
| **une barraque** | *dump, hole* |
| **un minet** **une minette** | *the sort of trendy type to be seen in the King's Road on Saturdays.* |

83

| | |
|---|---|
| une sèche | |
| un clope | |
| une pipe | |
| une tige | *cigarette, fag, straight* |
| une taf | *drag (of a cigarette)* |
| un verre | |
| un pot | *drink, jar* |
| payer un verre | *buy s.o. a drink* |

e.g.

Viens, je te paie un verre.

*Come on, I'll buy you a drink.*

| | |
|---|---|
| un jus | |
| un express | *black coffee in a tiny cup* |
| un jerk | *fast dance* |
| un slow | *slow music to grope to* |
| le rock | *jive (remember?)* |
| faire tapisserie | *be a wall flower* |
| draguer | *chat up, pick up* |

e.g.

Tu vois les deux nanas là-bas? On va les draguer, hein?

*See those two chicks over there. Let's chat them up.*

| | |
|---|---|
| ramasser une veste | *get refused a dance by a chick* |
| poser un lapin | *stand s.o. up* |

**tenir la bougie**    *play gooseberry*

e.g.

J'en ai marre de tenir la bougie. Je vais filer.

*I'm fed up with playing gooseberry. I'm going.*

**elle est bien roulée.**  *she's a doll*

**une allumeuse**
**une chaufe-cul**    *a P.T.*

**un orchestre**    *group*

e.g.

La boîte était moche, mais l'orchestre n'était pas mal.

*The club was rough, but the group wasn't bad.*

**un tube**    *hit record, smash hit*

**un videur**    *bouncer*

**un costeau**

**un malabar**
**une armoire-à-glace** *hard-case, neanderthal*

**barraqué**    *square set, tough looking*

**casser la gueule**    *beat s.o. up*

e.g.

Tu veux que je te casse la gueule?

*How'd you like a fat lip?*

## II   A LA FAC'

| | |
|---|---|
| **la Fac'** | *university, college* |
| **rentrer en Fac'** | *go up, back to college* |
| **les copains** | *your friends, mates* |
| **un prof'** | *teacher, lecturer, tutor* |
| **un bouquin** | *book* |
| **bouquiner** | *read* |
| **bosser** | |
| **bûcher** | *work, read for an essay* |
| **chialer** | *swot, gnome, read up* |
| **barber** | *bore* |
| **se barber** | *to be bored* |
| **barbant** | *boring* |
| **la flemme** | *laziness* |
| **avoir la flemme** | *be lazy, too lazy* |

e.g.

J'ai la flemme de bosser ce soir.

*I can't be bothered to work tonight.*

| | |
|---|---|
| **un flemmard** | *lazy sod* |
| **se la couler douce** | *have a soft time of it* |

| | |
|---|---|
| **avoir du cul** | |
| **avoir du pot** | *be jammy, lucky* |
| **manquer de cul** | |
| **manquer de pot** | *be unlucky* |
| **sècher** | *skip a lecture, course* |
| **tuisser** | |
| **pomper** | *crib, cheat in an exam* |
| **mordre** | *cheat* |
| **se faire saquer** | *get a bad mark* |
| **être recalé** | |
| **ramasser une banane** | |
| **prendre une veste** | *fail an exam* |
| **lècher** | |
| **failloter** | *suck up* |
| **un lèche-cul** | *toe-rag, crawler* |
| **un vieux schnok** | *gruesome wrinklie, old don* |
| **s'empiffrer** | *stuff one's face* |
| **un morphale** | *pig, glutton* |
| **les flics** | |
| **les poulets** | *the fuzz* |
| **passer à tabac** | *get duffed up (by the police)* |

# III  ABUSE

French abuse is highly colourful, relying more on
Irony and richness of imagery than plain filth, and
its translation into a more basic Anglo-saxon idiom
would not and could not do it justice. Therefore, in
this Appendix, I have restricted myself to an enumera-
tion of some of the more common expressions, with
notes on usage and meaning where these are necessary or helpful in any way. It only remains to reiter-
ate my warning about the fragile Froggy Ego. If
you are abusive, you can expect a violent reaction.
The Frog in the street is not used to taking abuse
lying down, or to ignoring the remarks of others
(unless, of course you are asking someone the way
etc.). Furthermore, the French sensibility is such
that someone is more likely to be offended by being
called a "sad case", than if you had impugned the
legitimacy of his forefathers for four generations.
Similarly, the Frog female is quite likely to clout
you over the head with her hand/shopping bag if
she thinks you're getting cocky, so beware.

However, enough warning: I shall start the list
with a note on that famous French expletive "merde".

**merde**

In French, this is really the only way of expressing
the myriad English ejaculations of a similar vein. In
order to give the word a greater or lesser expletive

value, the pronunciation is modulated. Thus, when said quietly and reflectively with no undue emphasis, it is unlikely to cause a great deal of offence. However, when given its full weight and uttered loudly and roundly, it will have considerably more effect.

It is possible to bolster the word with others, but this varies from one part of the country and one group of people to another; such forms exist as:

**merde de la bordel** (which is a dialect usage)
**putain bordel de merde**
or
**double merde**

There is considerable scope for originality of expression in this field, and with practice the nuances of usage become second nature.

As promised in Vocabulary List C, here are the nouns referring to men and women which are pejorative in character. In this list I shall give the closest equivalent English slang term, if such a term exists.

| | |
|---|---|
| **une baleine** | *boot, cow (plump girl usually* |
| **un boudin** | *below* 25) |
| **un dauphin** | |
| | |
| **un cachalot** | *scrawny chick* |
| **un cageot** | |
| | |
| **une conasse** | *dozy, thick bird* |
| **une greluche** | |
| | |
| **un tas de tôle** | *slag-heap, old boot (general* |
| | *term)* |

| | |
|---|---|
| une salope | *slut, bitch* |
| une garce | |
| une dégueulasse | |
| une gonzesse | *tarty bird (mutton dressed* |
| une poule | *up as lamb)* |
| une pute | *whore (actual or implied)* |
| un putain | |
| un pauvre type | *sad case* |
| un con | *berk, prick, stupid bastard* |
| un couillon | |
| un conard | |
| un morpion | |
| un emmerdeur | *pain in the arse, nuisance* |
| un salaud | *bastard (non-literal)* |
| un salopard | |
| un greluchon | |
| un maquereau | *ponce, pimp* |
| un mac' | |

If someone is annoying you, and you wish them to go away, there are many ways of expressing this request. I have split them into two basic groups, the Ironic and the openly abusive. Firstly the Ironic, which have no real English equivalents.

vas te faire voir
vas te faire chlorophyler
ramasse tes billes et vas jouer ailleurs

and there are many others. The openly abusive expressions are roughly equivalent to the English "... off", where the blank denotes some basic human activity:

vas te faire foutre
vas te faire baiser
vas te faire empapaouter
vas te faire enculer chez les grecs

Here again the scope for originality is considerable.

The following phrases convey that the person addressed is being a drag. They are very idiomatic, quite untranslatable and largely Ironic.

tu m'emmerdes
tu me dailles le pistil
tu me pèles le jonc
tu me fais chier
tu me les broutes
tu me les gonfles
tu me casses les couilles

These idioms convey that the person addressed is unattractive to you and probably everyone else. A facial characteristic is frequently parodied.

tu as un oeil qui dit merde à l'autre
tu as un nez à rayer le plancher
tu as une gueule à razer les murs
tu as une gueule en coin de rue
amène ta mère que je te refasse

And finally there are certain very complicated and coarse replies to the **"et ta soeur"** of Vocabulary List I. I list them below, but they seem too long and involved for easy use, and so I cite them as examples of the lengths the Frog will go to in this respect.

et ta soeur?
Elle bat le beurre. Et quand elle battera la merde, tu viendras me grignoter le bambou (*or* me sucer le bâton).

et ta soeur?
Elle pisse bleu. Et si tu as quelquechose à faire teindre, tu viendras me voir. Ça sera gratuit.

# IV THE ANATOMY LESSON

This is a list of certain terms of a predominantly physical nature, which tend to be omitted from most vocabularies, despite their frequent use in coarse conversation. They are, of course, to be used with a certain amount of caution, as they may shock the prurient, and thereby cause considerable embarrassment to the speaker. And we don't want these Froggy chappies getting a chance to make us look silly, do we?

| | |
|---|---|
| **foutre** | *copulate* |
| **baiser** | |
| **sabrer** | |
| **enculer** | *sodomise* |
| **empapaouter** | |
| **un pédé** | *queer, pansy, fairy* |
| **un pédale** | |
| **une tapette** | |
| **une gouine** | *lesbian* |
| **la queue** | *virile member* |
| **la bite** | |
| **la pine** | |
| **la balayette** | |
| **les couilles** | *testicles* |
| **les noyeaux** | |
| **les joyeuses** | |

| | |
|---|---|
| **la chagatte** | *female genitalia* |
| **le barbu** | |
| **le con** | |
| **les nichons** | *breasts* |
| **les nénés** | |
| **les roberts** | |
| **les tétons** | |
| **les chiottes** | *privy* |
| **chier** | *defecate* |
| **pisser** | *urinate* |
| **peloter** | *caress* |

# NOTES

# NOTES